REFLECTIONS

NAKED POETIC IMAGES VOLUME I

Sankora

Learn from the past

The original works of

Aisha D. DaCosta

as

ADDicted

Published by You Edition, March 2007

Copyright 2006 by Aisha D. DaCosta

ISBN   978-0-6151-4275-3

In a dark room
seated around tables
with lit candle centerpieces
they're dressed in all black
Can you hear them as they snap
fingers to your poetic tones?
Laid back in a hypnotic zone
from the back, one calls out
"Yeah, I'm feeling that!"
Welcome to...

REFLECTIONS

NAKED POETIC IMAGES VOLUME I

Poetry is more than a leisure pursuit it's an addiction...painting images with words. - ADDicted

Dedicated to my family, my
friends that have become
family, and everyone I have
ever loved in between.

FOREWORD

Looking back in retrospect, I guess I should have named this book "Evolution". The most profound thing that I've discovered as I read this compilation is the development of rhythm. I've never been a fan of my poetry, until recent years that is...I've always written for therapeutic purposes; trying desperately to make sense of those events that shape the human condition.

"Reflections" captures within its pages prose that spans over a decade. The earliest poem 'When the cage bird sings" dates back to my high school years, somewhere around 1995-1996. The latest poem "I'm in love" was composed in March 2007.

The poems authored during 2005-2007 have a distinct feel, an idiosyncratic rhythm. The composition of "Illicit" took place in 2006 while I was deployed at Baghdad, Iraq and solidified the evolution of Aisha DaCosta to ADDicted...Enjoy!

A mother's denial

From conception your warmth
Was the only thing known
Labor pains of birth
Have ignited emotions captive & torn
Nostalgic visions of a relationship lost
Have turned nurture to scorn
A child never thought of
Is unfortunately born
A father's name in ink
Has brought about a life void of love
For he was never around
And you're misunderstood
We all know you struggled
Were tortured and cried
But, you emotionally abandoned
A child who has committed no crime
Your sins are forgiven
Yet your apathy you deny
For this very reason at night
My heart still cries
I would ask for an explanation
To the question of why
But fear of your response
being desolate and dry
Has made me come to the realization
That you'll never search deep

Within to compose a reply
That will ever satisfy
As you fester in your maternal lie
My heart will forever be broken and
continuously cry

A sigh of relief

At one time I believed
Without you I would grieve
My eyes have been opened
Blessed by reality I see
Our love may not be forever
But it has taught me
That when you leave
I can still breathe
A sigh of relief
The greatest gift you have ever given me
Is the courage to move on
Our trials, tribulations,
arguments and fights
Have forged my spirit and
prepared me for this night
As I set free what I've loved for so long
My heart skips a beat
I release, a sigh of relief

Believe Me

They wouldn't believe me if I said,
I've loved you for years
To them it's inconceivable
That I am drenched by your tears
For when they look at you
They perceive only anger and rage
I've already read that chapter
And I am on the next page
Past your façade and insecurities
I see who you've been, who you are
And what you aspire to be
They see what you've done,
What you do
And they don't believe me
When I say that I love you
And will cherish you for eternity
Prejudged and misunderstood
Written off by the evils of history
To them, you are no more
than a wild beast
Rescued from the entangled
jungles of the East
To me, you are an
un-pressured diamond
Captive in coal and awaiting release
Blind to your beauty

and afraid of your worth
They will never believe me
If I said I've loved you from birth
Black man, black woman
Young minds under siege
Prisoner to discrepancies
Embedded in society
Love yourself as I love thee
Because they don't believe me

Black History

Remember me?
I'm your Black History!
I'm that drug dealer with bleach white
Uptown's on my feet
Pockets swoll like arthritic
feet in the heat
Side arm loaded, ready to cock
at a moment's notice
Remember me?
I'm your Black History!
I'm your Harriet Tubman, Malcolm X,
Marcus Garvey, slave ship survivor
Self-educated, single mother,
sole income provider,
mother and father to three
Working full-time and part-time

to make ends meet
Do you, do you remember me?
I'm your Black History!
I'm that 10-yr. old
that never made it to grade six
Gunned down in the streets
over some bullshit
Remember me, remember me?
I'm your Black History!
I'm that street poet begging for one mic
Staring up at the ceiling
before I go to sleep at night
Wishing that one day…one day I'll
make it out the hood
Get a record deal,
"Damn, everything'll be all good"
You see, I'm your Black History
I'm that lesson taught
left out of textbooks in school
That calculus problem
that makes you feel like a fool
The reason why you cut class
to hang outside the school
Do you…do you remember me?
I'm your Black History
I'm the Black Holocaust reparations
you will never get
I'm the Section 8 housing you

and your man live at
I'm that eviction notice
taped to the front door
The formula and diapers
you don't have money for
I'm that high school graduate
with aspirations of college
That enlisted in the Army because
mommy and daddy couldn't afford it
Do you...do you remember me?
I'm your Black History!

Can I kiss you?

Grant me permission
to touch you in ways
that'll tell stories about how I miss you
re-living the imagery of your presence
as you occupy my mind when I kiss you
Answer me now, as I wait
with baited breath...
Can I kiss you?
And paint pictures with my tongue
depicting lust enslaved by love
unshackling desire as we touch
pulling you closer, holding you tighter
'til our hearts beat as one
Can I kiss you?

Will the taste of your lips
set me free from my insomniac sleep?
Hoping the asylum that I seek
borders lie beyond your sheets
Beyond the eternal sensations
of each caress,
the ecstasy, the obsession
when I'm with you…
Can I kiss you?

Daddy's Little Girl

In the mirror she finds glimpses of him
the complexion of her skin,
the curls in her hair
the fullness of her lips,
sketches images of him
As she tries to reconcile
with never knowing him
Never knowing how it feels
to be daddy's little girl
She is forced to walk in a cold world
finding warmth and refuge
in another's arms
Learning that the silhouette
of derelict paternal obligations
craters the self-image
of neglected little girls

painting a distorted portrait of love
Daddy's little girl
grows up to be a woman
not quite healed,
camouflaging her face
with courage and strength
trying desperately to conceal the pain
hoping her façade will not reveal
that his vacancy still haunts
as it blemishes her glee
warping the way she receives
and dispenses love
Daddy's little girl
never knew the warmth of his hug
yet still chases the comfort of his love

Decisions of the heart

Command me with desire
as I fall victim to your waist
Taunt me with your lips,
while I yearn for their taste
With eyes wide shut,
I still see your face
Recognition of its resilience
makes me elate
In a moment of doubt,
I stop to ponder if this is fate?

Can emotions so wild, ever be tamed?
How will I conjure up the courage
to ask him his name?
Our love affair runs rapid,
as it exists in my head
Flourishes like a flower,
yet deaf to your voice
I realize one day;
I will have to make a choice
Ruin all that we have and take a chance
on love, or remain in the distance,
far from your embrace
Never to behold your spirit,
my life becomes a waste
Decisions of the heart, love and its chase
Mind over matter;
take a chance or waste

Ego Tripping

He says...
"Baby, tell me you love me"
every time we part
And I'm left wondering
if he can't feel the veracity of my heart
Is it not enough
that I've never loved
anyone as I do him

Are my kisses unable to convey
these feelings that I'm feeling
Translate kinetic emotions
into dreams of eternity
and erase from his mind
insecure manifestations,
doubts of devotion,
or is he just ego tripping?

Empty

I feel empty inside
although I've prayed and Cried
Hoping thAt today,
time will heal this paiN inside
I Can't undERstand why,
The young and beautiful die
My only sister, diagnosed and
died before the birth of my first Child
Who in the world comtemplAtes
death at 26?
ONe Can only fEel invincible
No one thinks this could be it
Life as we know it is oveR with
I CAN't stop Crying no mattER
how hard I try
I know it's unfair
to my husband and child

But some days I wish I died
At least then I won't hurt,
No longer would I cry
No longer would I feel empty inside!

Enemy in my bed

What is so captivating about
the look in his eyes?
What is it that pierces my soul
every time he smiles?
If I was to say, I don't, never did,
never will ever care
It would be in attempt to disguise
feelings that I fear
or maybe I'm just scared
that what haunts me
Is a nightmare we don't share
If so, let it be for I never really cared
Emotions once confessed
no longer live here
It was all a ploy, to lure him near
Break down every wall;
strip his heart naked and bare
In his vacancy I profess, I never did care
Yet when I am alone with my thoughts
His footprints are still clear
Love's paradox ignites

anger and despair
As my body shakes from withdrawal
and fever takes hold
To everyone that will listen
this story is told…
Beware of his smile and
the deceit it holds
Run far from his touch,
its grasp is cold
Never look in his eyes,
for his heart is stone
Such a glance will cost you,
everything you own
Stay clear of his bed,
its sheets are decapitating
Resist words of lust
that feel emancipating
Fall deaf to his song and
each seductive verse
Or you too will be inflicted
by love's evil curse
I wish the words that I speak
were spoken to me
For if they were maybe then
I would have seen
That what I lured in my bed,
sought to destroy me

EYES

Their intensity pierces my soul
As I, long to hold your hand
letting this pain in my chest
run like electric currency
from my heart to your soul
when you look at me

I wonder if you know
My hearts skips a beat with every stare
then speeds up to compensate
for rhythm lost
with each glance, each stare
The music locked in those eyes
serenades my soul as they bind

Is this chaos intentional?
Some primal communication
like Navajo smoke signals
Conveying a message lost
in verbal translation
when you talk to me

Your eyes, your eyes
Damn, they consume me
and pressure me to engage
you in conversation

about what you are doing to me
but, I'm scared, so scared, that…
you're looking at someone behind me

Fraternal Tears

Sometimes it's amazing
the things life causes us to see
There is nothing more eye opening
than the fraternal tears
that you've cried for me
When anger consumes
I feel only my pain
I've never stopped to think
if you feel the same
Maybe it was my own vanity
that has caused me to abstain
from the expression of feelings that
oppress like shackles and chains
Be it as it may, my sister your tears
were not in vain
for they have caused me to see
that I am not the only one in pain,
not the only one that hurts, there are
others that feel the same
And so begins my shame like the
nakedness of Adam and Eve
unfortunately it took your tears

for me to look beyond me
all apologies aside
We are charged to love
to love each other
Another woman as a sister
sometimes maybe even as a mother
But how can that be
where am I to find love for someone
that looks nothing like me?
We are women of different
genetic codes,
eyes and skin tones
I'll explain it to you once
The answer is in the EAST
Look upon a STAR when
your journey seems too far
burden too heavy to bare
call out I'll be there
Your heart's every whisper
I'll listen when no one else cares to hear
Rest assured your fraternal tears
were not wasted
For sister I am here!

Fraternal Woes

Fofo

Jealousy, envy

My sista, my soror, my friend
Lend me your ear
I have a question to ask,
Do you really care?
Picture me broken with a burden
Too heavy to bare
Will you carry my cross, or
stand there and stare?
Spectator or friend
Where are you to find?
Are you standing by my side,
or deaf to my cry?
MY SISTA, MY SOROR,
MY FRIEND (sigh)
Let me begin again,

With open arms you greet me
As you embrace me with envy
Painfully you kiss me
While you hide your deceit
We were taught to be humble
With my hair I wash your feet
Even Jesus had his Judas
So sisterly I greet
For I understand that you are blind,
Feeble minded and weak
Know nothing of sisterhood
And have never nursed scorched feet
For it's the burning sands
that I've crossed
That make me feel so deep
For I am my sister's keeper
So I address you
from shepherd to sheep
My sista, my soror, my friend
Hate not that which
you can not comprehend
Love those who are lost
As a SISTA, a SOROR, a FRIEND

Ghetto Song

I want to sing a ghetto song
About these ghettos that
were once occupied
by Jewish niggers that have since
emancipated themselves,
but are now filled with
this precarious breed of
black niggers that enslave themselves
Fighting, killing, pimping, hoeing
For a piece of that American pie
War criminals they are
guilty of generational genocide
As they poison the minds
of their children with media lies
Hoop dreams, Cutlass Supremes,
Collegiate ambitions
labeled as bourgeoisie
With adolescent praise of the streets
They speak, eat, and drink
The foul retched stench of their own shit
As they pretend there is nothing wrong
With falling victim to this ghetto song
Chastised intellectuals,
glorified criminals
lost individuals need to hear this song
This ghetto song

Ghost of Djembe

I know I'm not deaf
I can hear the rhythm
I can feel the beat
But, my feet won't move
to the music
You see there used to be
steps outlined for my feet
Impressions made by the footsteps
of my ancestors as they speak
We've lost the groove
That jazz, the rhythm,
the way we used to move
That sway as we danced to
The beats of djembe

Hard-headed

I agonize over words not said
They're right, I'm hard headed
Because I can't get it through my head
It's hard to fathom that
you're really gone
My son, my heart, my love
And you weren't there
I wish I could have shared that moment
The pain I bear, the fears, the tears

I wish you could see him now
He smiles like you
Something called sunshine
The way he brightens up the room
I miss you
I love you
I'm tortured
I'm torn
I'm here
And I still can't believe you're gone

Have you heard?

Have you ever heard
the day break
and the darkness shatter
in the sunrise?

Have you ever heard
the rolling thunder of tears,
the clap of their fall,
the crumble of walls
as the heart cries?

Have you ever heard
the laughter of love
as pain's intensity fades?

Have you heard
the world around you
as it dies, as it grows?
Have you ever heard?

I can't get you out of my head

I-can't-get-you-out-of-my-head
My heart calls out your name
Like I miss you or some shit
Then, right before I break down and cry
My brain kicks in endorphins
To dull the pain and
stops me from going insane
But let's keep it real because…
I-can't-get you-out-of-my-head
I can still feel your touch
when I lay in my bed
So, I tried this yoga shit
and stood on my head
Trying to repress any thoughts of you
But, all I accomplished was blood loss
to my legs and thighs
Damn, I-can't-get-you-out-of-my-head
Yesterday, I went to the salon
 for one of those Angela Bassett,
Waiting to Exhale haircuts

I am almost bald like Erica Badu
And the shit didn't work
because I still think about you
I-can't-get-you-out-of-my-head
So, tonight I'm meeting Joe
at the club for drinks
Maybe, he'll think I'm sexy
and we'll mentally click
Go back to his place to watch a flick
But, what if I wake up in his bed
And start to think about you
And reminisce about how
we used to make love
Damn! I-can't-get-you-out-of-my-head
So instead of risking it all
on a one night stand
I'll stand guard by the phone
anticipating your phone call
Hoping we can somehow make up,
And you are NOT the same asshole that
caused us to break-up
You know what, I'll just move on and
pretend like your dead
Who am I kidding?
I-can't-get-you-out-of-my-head

If I...

If I could take back all
the harsh words spoken, I would
If I could regain your trust again,
I would
If I could stop your heart from breaking,
I would
If I only understood
what you meant to me
We would, still be in love
If I could, take back all the pain,
I would
But, we were too young
and I misunderstood
But, if I could,
I would love you again
Now that it's understood
As I rationalize and
say it's for our own good
Deep down I know
I misunderstood
The wrongs I did
can never be made good
Although I now realize
I misunderstood
If I only could,
I would

Illicit

His name must remain anonymous
so I'll call him Illicit
Desire often delivers me
to the crossroads
of reality and imagination
Beckoning me closer and closer
to the outskirts of temptation
Coercing me…this persuasive devil's
whisperings plays center stage,
my romantic Iago
Painting visions of
reconquista over the Moor
Adding fuel to my yearning;
provoking lust more and more
and when I think of him,
this prohibited creature
the imagery he illustrates
in my mind must be
categorized as explicit
I can't reveal his name
so I'll just call him Illicit

I'm in love

I'm in love again
But this time it's different
from the last time
This time it feels like the first time
I've ever been in love
Ever kissed
Ever hugged
Ever touched without being touched
I'm in love
And my soul speaks
the thoughts of my heart
Singing love songs like
"I can't breathe without you" songs
"You mean the world to me" songs
"I will always love you" songs
That sound like the only song
I was ever meant to sing
And when you kiss me
Kiss me mouth open,
Soul open,
Tongue saturated with love
Can you taste it?
I'm in love

Islam

The vitality of this heart
as it beats like a drum
vibrations emancipated through
the understanding of Islam
Head covered, with a soul halal
No wine, no pork, no fornication of love
Dedication so pure, devotion for one
None enjoined in the remembrance of
Thirty-three by three
Ninety-nine times as we
Pray five times
On hands and knees
The illustration of faith
Pressed in the bosom of love
Nourishment provided by its milk
Morality revealed by nakedness guilt
Free as the will to think
On a foundation of faith Islam is built

I want to write poems

I want to write poems
about big girls I used to tease
and send out apologizes
about the way I made them feel
Like Ode to a Big Girl, I'm sorry!

And I guess for ugly girls
I'm going to have to write Part II

I want to write poems about poems
that make you want to cry
about secrets and lies
that you've tried to hide

I want to write poems about
high school girls
for the baby inside that she let die
because she was too scared
to tell her mother why

I want to write poems about
a mother's denial
And explain to the world why
I can't hug her no matter how hard I try

I want to write poems and write poems
And write poems and write poems
Tell stories and lies, truth and denials

I want to write poems about love,
poems about hate
Poems about sorrow, poems about fate
I want to write poems about marriage,
divorce and debate

Topics that stir up feelings of hate

I want to write poems so abstract
Only I can relate
Like, there were these birds,
pigeons, horses that fly
in this big ol' ménage a trois in the sky
I want to write poems
I want to write poems
I want to write poems

Invisible Emotions

Boundless words of admiration
are held captive in my throat
Exposure of their sincerity
would cause pride to revolt
So I have chosen to disguise
the glimmer in my eye
That is ignited every time you smile
I've loved you from a far
for what seems like an eternity
The harmonic melody
of your voice gives me serenity
When life renders me helpless and weak
Sometimes all I desire
is to hear you speak
Now answer me this

Am I absolutely insane
for feeling this way
For a man, who has no name?
Before I am committed, let me explain…
The day we first met
it was as if my life started all over again
My Alpha and Omega
has given me a love that provokes envy
in the greatest of men
The authenticity of such emotions
is often overpowering
At very least mind-boggling
Before all on earth I profess
that what I feel inside is bona fide,
void of deceit, jealously, and rage
A love so pure is virgin in nature
Often sought, rarely achieved
Written off as make-believe
Invisible emotions, they bind me

Just Because

It's 6pm and he's late coming home
His bath water gets cold
As I sprinkle rose petals on the floor
I can't wait
Until he comes through the door
His look alone will be enough

You see my man, he's had it rough
Somewhere in between
12 hr shifts and overtime
He has to find the energy to love me
The same way he did the first time
We enjoined souls and became one
Get up, take a shower
And be a father to our son
Then figure out new ways
to tell me he loves me
And convince me I'm still the one
So, tonight
Just because I'm in love
Just because I'm glad he's my husband
My man, a father to our son
With my hair I'll wash his feet
Dry off his body with my tongue
Whisper erotic verses as we
Embrace in a long awaited hug and
We'll make love
Just because

Kiss

A collaborative work
By ADDicted & NDru (N. Andrew DaCosta)

I'm watching his eyes
roll back into his head
Wondering what it is exactly
that he's feeling
Pondering for just a moment
The feeling of my lips against his
And the passion it stirs in him
What if I could feel those
same orgasmic sensations
that cause him to quiver
from every touch my fingers deliver
Would my kisses evoke in me
the same rides of emotion
ever so gently killing him softly,
leaving him yearning for these lips
that I've known for so long?
Ahh, and when our lips finally meet
He speaks of desire burning so deeply
Searing every nerve
throughout his body
until he becomes numb
When greeted with my tongue,
he says he can taste
his heart as it melts

And from the feeling of his chest
against mine
I can tell his heart
skipped a beat when he kissed me

Kiss me, like you
just fell in love with me
I can tell you love me by
how you kiss me
Not that superficial mundane kiss
one gets when we greet
Give me that, you could hardly
wait to press your soft wet lips
into my soul, kiss
I swear sometimes that kiss
makes my whole body orgasm
in delight
You know, it's that feeling that
you really love me,
you really adore me,
you really miss me,
even if we are apart for only one day
Looking out the window,
watching as you
walk from the street
and at the door we meet
Oh God! that first kiss
Like I was gonna die without it

Or, relaxing on the sofa
and your head resting in my lap,
that very first kiss before we make love.
Electric!!!
I just want to be kissed...like that,
always like that.

Leadership

Nea Ope Se Obedi Hene
    Service, leadership

Night after night I've dreamt
this fearful dream
Faces unfamiliar within
a reoccurring scene
Entertain for just a minute this
metaphor as a theme,
Leader as a ship docked

or stranded at sea.
Commander of a vessel
most foreign to me
Navigator equipped with compass,
unable to read
You see, I know what it is to be led
But do I have what it takes to lead?
If all that was ever known as reality
shattered to make-believe
Would I have what it takes
to illuminate the disbelief?
In the midst of destruction, to another's
pain could I bring reprieve?
Leader as a ship docked
or stranded at sea
At the dock of bay, I have stormed harsh
weather and finally found my way
Half full, half-empty, stranded at sea
From either perspective you're in place
you shouldn't be
You see, I know what it is to be led
But do I have what it takes to lead?
Define it you can, alphabetically
letter by letter in Webster's dictionary
You can even practice its movements
with drill and ceremony
But until your heart beats to its rhythm
And your mind fathoms its reason

You will forever be,
leader as a ship stranded at sea

Lonely Solider

Oceanic puddles of sorrow reflect
Empty M-16 magazines
that used to display
pornographic scenes
Of sadistic love making
on foreign battlefields

I'm a lonely soldier
Caught in between AEF rotations
And childhood dreams
Borrowed frustrations
of birthdays past,
anniversaries to come,
presents lost in the mail
And desert fun

Still nights I cry myself to sleep
Cuddled in between sheets
That bring no comfort to me
As I steal glances of
Faded pictures snuggled in between
Biblical verses that fail to bring reprieve
from this loneliness that tortures me

As I drop to my knees
Hear this lonely soldier speak
Dear God, can you hear me?

Love Poem #1

This thing beating harder
than the thundering clap of drums
calling to freedom runaway slaves
RUN…FASTER…HARDER…RUN!
Smile…laugh…a hug…a kiss…a glance
They call it love

Love Poem #2

I remember back when we used to
make love on a twin-sized mattress
it seemed much easier then…
staying in love paycheck to paycheck
between $1.25 slices of pizza and fries
subsidized metro transit rides
forgiving your lies
seemed much simpler then…
back when

Lust

An emotion too often confused with love

I must fore warn
the expression of these thoughts
are absolutely sincere
For recently I find myself infatuated
by your smile
imprisoned by your eyes
with a touch so erotic
I am driven absolutely wild
Pardon me if I stare
but I am in love with your waistline,
the way you walk,
the movement of your hips,
the thickness of your manhood,
the way you kiss my lips
But, does it stop there?
Is sex the only thing we share?
Do you miss me when I'm not there?
When you close your eyes,
do I still exist in your head?
Or is my silhouette only sketched in
your bed?

Mother of the revolution

Akokonan
Mercy, nurturing

I want to give birth to
the next black revolution
For I've grown tried
of old Negro spirituals
Verses of freedom songs
Faded memories of revolution
Neatly tucked away in "we shall
overcome" melodies
I'm ready for my people to rise up
Rise up and revolt
Revolt against the self-destructive
psychological programming
we have forced fed
ourselves for generations
and generations and generations

Rise up and give life to this long
overdue revolution
So that our struggles will be done
And we can finally overcome
the narcotic pollution of our mind, body
and soul that has pacified us for years
Don't get me wrong
I'm no black militant, afro-picking, black
t-shirt wearing extremist
trying to overthrow
the government and such
I'm just a single mother raising a son
That will taste pain I've never tasted
And face far more struggles than I'm
equipped to prepare him for
It takes a village to raise a child
And only the outset of revolution,
Yes the birth of a black revolution
Can save my son
from media brainwashing,
scholastic miseducation
the rampant spread of
plantation politics
the inevitable status of
second-class citizen
the tiresome chase of this rat race
that I've grown so tired of
I want to be the mother

of the next black revolution
So that my son isn't suffocated
by the terms of his birth
Or conditioned by
the colonial bullshit taught in school
And yes I'll teach him
about African kings,
help him unlock the kinetic
power of his ancestors
that lays dormant within
out-stretch the boundaries
of his ambitions beyond
21st century Jim Crow laws and MTV
I'll join Martin and Malcolm
on the mountain top
screaming at the height of my lungs
for revolution, revolution,
a black revolution!

Motherhood

Conversation interrupted
Water left broken on the floor
Suitcase in hand as we rush out the door
Thirty minutes of highway
to the glass doors
Entrance finally achieved
Through an open side door

Elevator going up
Labor and Delivery, Third Floor
24 hours of waiting
1 hour of pushing
For a second my heart stopped
as I pause to hear
Wait no more, lungs are cleared
40 weeks later, you're finally here

My Child

When the doctor announced
that I was with child,
I was filled with joy yet
I sat there and cried
I prayed for this moment
when I said I do
When reality hit I was consumed
Here I sit faced with raising a child
beautiful and divine
Can I provide those things
I was denied?
Will I kiss him enough?
Or cause him to cry?
Can I fortify his heart
and make it as strong as mine?
Or will he fall victim
as I watch in despair?

All praises to Allah
for this seed inside
Dear GOD give me the strength
to raise my child!

My Girl Friends

Late night calls when I could not sleep
I woke you out yours so
WE could count sheep
My…girl…friend
At times separated by roads that bend
Or oceans with floors
one can not descend
Phone calls connected by Operator 10
Lengthy e-mails that seem to never end
You've always been, my…girl…friend
Remember, when I lost girlfriend #1
My sister, my soror, my best friend
You were there as I shed tears
Over photos and thoughts
Constantly giving the comfort
I thought I lost
My…girl…friend
Always there through thick and thin
No win situations,
the bright tunnel at the end
My…girl…friend

When I trip and brace myself for the fall
You've always picked me up
Before my hand hits the floor
You are my…girl…friend!

My Love

Donde es mi amor?
Papi, ven aqui
Ven aqui, and rescue me
I've tried to capture words
To express my longing for
But, I am still wondering
Where you are?
Who you are?
My soul mate that I've
Searched for, for so long
Guapo, alto, negro you are
Papi, ven aqui!
Kiss me, mi amor

Not the same

Dedicated to Niles, Nicki II, Neville, Nefertiti
and Nicki

"Good morning, my love"
A wet kiss on the cheek
"Tie your shoelaces now,

before you trip on your feet"
A scene rehearsed, 365 times
Flawlessly executed,
on the drop of a dime
Love's indulgent embrace,
re-mastered the day you died
I held my head up high,
just like you taught
while inside I cried
I'm tripping, I'm drowning
I can't understand why
Too young to be consumed by pain
yet, too proud to cry
The hurt and pain remains the same
Dad, he tries his best
But, his kisses are rougher than yours
Birthdays and holidays
just aren't the same
We have five t-shirts in black
Imprinted with your dates and name
We miss you mom
Things just aren't the same

Pain

Nerves serve the senses,
like a ticketed line
Pain takes a number

to compose heartache's rhyme
If it wasn't for life
none would be
The pain and strife combine
to direct the flow
Traffic signal lights
permit emotions to go
out of control
as pain directs the flow

Papi Chulo

Each moment entwined in embrace
is shrouded with mystery
When you receive me, you hug me
as if you're trying to convey
more than "hello" as you greet me
Voices cry out in my mind…ooh Papi!
Damn, Papi!
Papi Chulo!
It's unbeknownst to you
what you're doing to me
Wild rides of emotion
as we touch…ooh Papi!
And when you depart from me
I wonder if you can hear
my heart calling out to you
Papi! Papi!

Ven aquí! Ven aquí!
Damn, Papi!
Papi Chulo!
If he only knew
I wonder what he would do…
I find myself the weakest
when it's only him and I in the room
and he's wrapping words in español
as if he's not the only one
that's bilingual
And all I can do is smile
I smile so wide
trying to hide my Achilles'
Avoiding contact with his eyes
Praying he doesn't hear my heart
as it cries
Ooh Papi!
Damn, Papi!
Papi Chulo!

Patri…who?

With laws constructed that separated
men whole from three fifths of a man
You call yourself patriotic
Patri…who? I don't understand!

When war broke out
and the North was in danger
of being severed from the South
Where did you look for the extra clout
to protect the Union
our founding fathers
so passionately wrote about?

When terrorists hooded
themselves in the South
Did you not feel my pain
or hear me cry out?
I called out for those
who fought by my side,
with my father and my uncle
for this country's pride
Where is your patriotism now,
when its my children
who need to be healed?
Did you leave it in Gettysburg
on its battlefield?

How can you honor in your heart what
you know to be a lie?
In your preamble,
did you constitute my cry?
Emancipate my sorrow? Or ratify a lie?

Yet you call yourself patriotic,
Patri...who?
I don't understand, why!

Poetry is...

Poetry is, what love is not
Liberated thoughts,
free from hatred's plot
Poetry is, like making love
with the sea between your legs
Poetry is, humble like the poor
that refuses to beg
and instead looks to God
for his daily bread
Poetry is, like telling time without a
clock or maybe it's the last
beat of the heart
before the blood flow stops
Poetry forgives pain,
as the mind blocks it out
Poets sketch words
that cry out "forget me not!"

Pork eating Muslim

Your ignorance escapes you
as it invades my privacy

In reply I greet you,
As-Salaamu Alaikum
Peace be unto you because
I don't know if I should slap you
or pray for you!

You have the audacity to ask
if I'm a pork eating Muslim
Now, I might not be a "do the right
thing" all the time Muslim
But, I'm try to pray
five times a day Muslim
I'm a fast during Ramadan Muslim
I'm a non-alcoholic drinking Muslim
I'm a I won't marry a Christian Muslim
And yes, just because you asked,
I'm a no pork eating Muslim

Not to be confused with a strap a bomb
on my chest Muslim
Or a jihad screaming Muslim,
because I disagree
with your policies Muslim
Nor am I a 1 of 4 wives Muslim

And remind me again
Who you are to ask
what kind of Muslim I am?

Please recapture your ignorance
and next time keep it to yourself!

Recipe of a Soror

DEFINITION OF HER TWENTY PEARLS

Compose her voice from eclectic notes
of truth and devotion
in a crescendo tone that soars heights
above treble or bass
exceeding the capacity
and weight of any clef
Gently chisel in her face
a womanly grace
that mimics the delicacy of rose petals
and emulates the beauty
protected by its thorns
On her shoulders endow
the strength of nations
for the globe gives curve to her back
as she is destined to lead and epitomize
the hopes and dreams of the
impoverished and unclean
Bestow upon her stride
the elegance and grace
of a swan as it glides
inject in each thigh pride and power
so that her majesty can stand tall

and capture her eminence in its shadow
Restrict her not by characteristic of race
nor bind her dimensions
to a predetermined frame
judge her worth to possess this name
repetitive of "A" separated by "K"
by the content of her heart, so that she
may lead the way

Religion

Gye Nyame
Supremacy of God

When a heart is in search
of a spiritual essence to behold
Life's discrepancies are challenged
as questions unfold

In what doctrine must one look,
for the answers to be whole?
Many profess knowledge
yet are lost in the cold
A reality void of reason
Enough to comfort the soul
Prayers left unanswered
Half the story never told

SMILE

Teeth so white
I can see you baby
When I turn out the lights
Your smile is captivating
Daddy enslave me
Tie me to the bed
Shackle and chain me
Whip me with your tongue
'til you've tamed me
And when you're done
Just smile at me

Still in love

Some nights I stare at the red light
on my answering machine
Blinking my eyes real fast, pressing play

Just to pretend you left
a message for me
Like "Hey Boo,
I just called to say I love you;
have a nice day", but in reality
There's this man talking about
"You have no new messages"
So I lay in my bed trying not
to think about you
Only to find myself tossing and turning
blowing kisses at
your picture on the wall
Before I know it
I feel this hand moving up my thigh
And just as it touches me
in ways you used to I realize
Damn, it's mine
Frantically searching
for toys under my bed
Only to find that my batteries are dead
And the truth is,
I'm still in love with you

Still Missing You

A collaborative work
By ADDicted and NDru

I have this broken record
playing in my head
Voices screaming I miss you, I miss you,
I can't believe your …
I can't even bring myself
to say that you're dead
The reality of those four letters is
messing with my head
It's been almost two years
since you've been gone
And I still hurt the same,
I still cry the same
There's something missing in my smile
Without calling your name

The world seems less bright now, more
dim, more dusty, more dirty.
I find myself calling out to you, as loud
as I can, if only in my head.
I'm hoping if a scream
your name loud enough,
you will eventually answer:
"Why are you yelling,
I'm right here stupid."

The reply that will keep this madness
from taking control of me.
Oh the abyss, the abyss!!!

I miss the warmth of your hugs
The sincerity laced in your kiss, the soul
piercing honesty you gave
Your energy is still missed
I close my eyes if only to catch a glimpse
Of your silhouette
as you run across my mind
Time stands still as I reminisce
Laughing and smiling to myself
in attempts to dull the pain
that pushes me closer to insanity
And rainy days
oh, these rainy days
just aren't the same
I cry to myself wishing the rain
will wash the tears from my day

If it were only so simple.
But, tears won't wash away tears.
Leaving, instead, the salty wet fears,
that I will continue to
lose all that I find dear.
One by one, will I lose what's left of my
crumbling serenity?

Will I have to compose
another elegant elegy?
I'm still playing hide-go-seek
with the reality,
trying to maintain, that stiff upper-lip.
And yes I miss those smart-mouth
quips, from your razor-sharp wit!

If only to hear the phone ring at 6am
on a Saturday morning
Tell the devil I will sell my soul
just to fumble in the dark
trying to receive
the morning cheer in your voice
Secretly wishing that you cared
about coastal time differences
and the fact I just
walked through the door
I miss you more than time can ever heal
The truth is, I never want
to feel like its okay
And that someday, somehow
miraculously this void
in my heart will one day disappear
I want nothing more than to miss you
Increasingly year after year

Strobe light Thing

We negotiated terms of romance
As we slow danced
To this Kama Sutra groove
Daddy, I'm not sure what it is
But, there's something about you
I mean like, I barely even know you
And I think
I'm falling in love with you
I guess it was a strobe light thing
See we met at the club,
I smiled, he laughed, we fell in love
I guess it was a strobe light thing
As minutes turned into hours
Hours turned into days
Days turned into weeks
I began to see
This wolf that played sheep
Un-dressing me with his eyes
Pulling me closer while
clinching my thighs
He conversed with me
in dialogue from hunter to prey
He knew what to say,
when to say it to get his way
Maestro of desire composing harmonic
melodies laced with sweet lies

He played fiddler with
the strings of my heart
As I re-wrote novels by Chinua Achebe
Things fall apart
And nothing was as it should be
I guess it was a strobe light thing
See we met at the club,
I smiled, he laughed, we fell in love
I guess it was a strobe light thing
Dreams of eternity
Became nightmares that
I can never convince myself
to be just that
In the aftermath of unrequited love
Will I ever trust again?
Will I ever love again?
Will I ever be more than one?
I guess it was a strobe light thing

Take 2

Arms embraced, hearts start to race,
a kiss on the cheek
"OUCH! You stepped on my feet."
REWIND; PLAY BACK
Every time we meet
"I love you"
"Me too"

"Hey, be good!"
As I thought to myself...
"I wish I could"
REWIND; PAUSE
I wish we never had to part
I miss my sister, my soror, my friend
I even miss your foot in my behind
You telling me what to do
Repeating my business
to people I never knew
Always opinionated
Sometimes too strong
Your way or the highway
We had to be wrong
Your absence has taken
its toll on mommy
She misses you too
She misses the baby she carried
for nine exhausting months
The toddler that was "grown"
before she could talk
That inquisitive child
that questioned the world
The teenager that never
took the easy way out
The young woman who
moved out on her own
The friend on the other end of the phone

Sunday morning conversations
And those late night talks
I know deep down she also misses the
arguments and fights
"You can't stay out late,
you're too young to date,
where the hell is my car,
this time you went too damn far"
Now, you're just not here at all
Without you, everything seems
like its wrong
Is this the way GOD meant it to be?
Did we follow the script?
I'm still waiting to hear….
LIFE, TAKE 2, ACTION
This can't be it!

Tears

My tears are reserved
for this pain inside
A pain so terrifying that I shake as I cry
To weak to bear its burden
So I lock it inside
"How are you doing, my dear?"
"I'm doing fine"
Your question, my reply

As I continue to lie
Who are you to inquire
about that which I deny?
Take my answer as truth
As I silently cry
And find comfort
In these lonely tears of mine

That Kinda Love

A collaborative work
By ADDicted and NDru

Sometimes I love my man like,
we can share the same toothbrush
kinda love
You know like if I fart on his leg
he won't get mad kinda of love
He'll just be like,
Ooh, girl you so silly kinda love
Sometimes I love him like
"damn you make me mad" kinda love
But, the best times
is when we make up kinda love

I seek that mind numbing kinda love
That, oh my God, kinda love
I want to bath in it kinda love
Rub it into my skin like Vaseline,

Cause I am dry without it kinda love
Be sick and infected by it kinda love
I want that nasty salacious kinda love,
but only between us kinda love

I'm looking for that
medicating kinda love
Take two kisses and a hug
Just to make it through
my day kinda love
While my nights are spent seeking
for that respirating kinda love
you know, like if I don't get it
I'll just die kinda love
So I replicate it
with every man I meet kinda love
Hoping that one day
I'll find that I love him
More than I love myself kinda love

The kinda love that makes me wanna
be unhappy and alone
rather than be in love and miserable
is not the kinda love I'm talking about
I'm talking about that
nervous feeling you get in your stomach
kinda love, makes me wanna throw-up
kinda love,

that sweaty, in the darkest corner,
grinding for dear life
kinda love, messing up our draws
kinda love,
that most intense adolescent kinda love

You know like that passing notes with
Circle yes or no if you like me
kinda love
Or that give me a hug
while I squeeze you butt kinda love
I want that kinda love that makes me do
Jumping Jacks naked just to make you
laugh kinda love

This Ramadan will be different

This Ramadan will be different
I won't fast the same
I'll pray a little harder
Fast a little longer
Cry more somber
Speak a little softer
Withdraw a little farther
Because this year's been rough!
How can you lose
the only sister you have

Give birth to your first child and
Leave your husband
in the span of eight months
And not pray a little harder
Fast a little longer
Cry more somber
Speak a little softer
And withdraw a little farther
This year Ramadan will be different
This year it starts on October 15th
She would be 27 if she were still here
It's been less than a year since she past
And this year of all years Ramadan
starts on October 15th
As if my year hasn't been hard enough
This year when I fast
I'll be reminded she's gone
This Ramadan will be different
And that's an understatement
I won't even blaspheme and say what
I've thought in my head
If it don't break you, it will make you
At least that's what they say
All I know is, this year,
Ramadan won't be the same!

To my son

Five times a day
I pray as hard as I can
to be an example for him
Every Bismillaah ir rahmaan ir raheem
I pray for my sins
I pray for GOD to protect him
You see, I loved him before I met him
Now, that I know him,
I'm in love again
My son
I will always be your first kiss
Your first love
As long as, we both shall live
Now, I reminisce about the
9 months that bought us to this
And the stretches that mark
My stomach, hips and thighs
I am filled with pride
as I look at my child
My son, My heart,
my love, the reason I exist
Always, always remember this….
I love you and I will always cherish
Every smile, every laugh, every kiss
As I reminisce
My son

To the younger me...

A collaborative work
By NDru and ADDicted

I am sending a message
to my younger self:
I know you well
so listen up
to what I have to tell
I want you to learn
the very best you can
because I now know
you will need it all
to succeed
I want you to heed
the warnings
of those older than you
apply their knowledge
to your situation
And, in Love:
never accept less
than love and respect
and, never ever hurt
the ones you love

As I sit here trying to compose a letter
Address to my younger self
Questions begin to unfold...

You know sometimes I wonder,
if no one ever said they loved me,
would I not still love myself?
Is sex the only means I possess to
express myself?
If no one ever said I was beautiful
Would I only have the absence
of love to define myself?
I wonder how many times
I will say I do,
Before I commit to loving someone
other than me, myself and I?
Are my relationship issues merely an
outgrowth of my parental issues?
Will all this confusion later lead to some
serious mental issues?
Damn, I've finished my last box of
Kleenex tissues only to realize
I still don't know how to address you
and the only words of wisdom I have
written of this white page is
I LOVE YOU!

Valentine

I didn't know what to get you
for Valentine's
So I decide to give you

a piece of my mind
Imagine this, a kiss from behind
Hands wrapped around your waist
As I whisper these thoughts of mine
I love…waking up… next to you
I miss…talking to you
I wish…I wish…I…never…lose you
I didn't know what to get you for
Valentine's Day
So I decide to tell you "I love you"
in a different way
Sunday Football, no interruptions,
breakfast in bed
See, I just want to…I just want to…
get in your head
A dozen red roses…..My man
Telegrams written in a romantic tongue
"To mi amor...te amo"...My man
How to express these feelings void of
chocolate teddy bear love
Wrap these emotions
in a passionate hug
Sealed with a kiss, climaxed with trust
I didn't know what to get you
for Valentine's
So I decided to send my love

WALK

The power of your legs
Intoxicates with every step
I wish you would stand still
So I can catch my breath
Close my eyes
Press rewind
Replay the image
Over and over again
Until I've memorized the
Movement of your hips
As the muscles in your legs
Perfectly sketched in your skin
Call out to me, teasing me
Encouraging my touch
As if, I haven't had enough

What if?
A collaborative work
By ADDicted and NDru

What if my mother
would have went to the clinic
and repented for the sin
her and my father repeated
over and over and over again?
Shameless desire turned bastard lust

captured by each selfish thrust
Manifestation,
this infant eradicating clinic visit
Would the world be any different?
If I was never given
the chance to be me?
Nor was I reincarnated
into someone else
What if?

I feel you little sister.
I'm your brother,
but I only share half your genes
What if he didn't capture my mother's
heart, the way he did yours,
like an insatiable predator
needing fresh meat,
never quenching his hunger,
or his childish Ego?
Letting his Id run wild and untamed,
crashing lives against his wake?
What if she didn't freeze from his lustful
gaze, would I be?
What if she couldn't conceive me in her
dreams? Would I breathe?
What if the mixture of their lovemaking
was a recipe for Armageddon?

What if I was never meant to see
daylight, sunsets, and glee?
What if that's the answer to me feeling
incorrect, out of place, and not of this
time and space?
What of me?

When I'm loving you

A collaborative work
By ADDicted and NDru

I want to kiss you with the
strength of every breath inside of me
Finding refuge in the ecstasy
You incite in me
I'll steal away for just a moment
Your breath so that I may breathe again
When I'm loving you

To you I'll confess my every sin
so that you may know
how far I've traveled
just to be with you
Express I will with every touch
that I'm in love with you
Feeling your heart pulsate next to mine
When I'm loving you

Have you no mercy?
The cruelty of that look,
paralyzes my mouth,
and I can't speak
I can only motion
for you to touch me
But, I am afraid of your touch,
not to my skin,
to my soul,
When I'm loving you

Can you save me,
from this empty wetness,
pooling my tears like blood?
Can you strike a deal
with the devil,
so I can be redeemed?
Am I redeemable? Am I lovable?
Show me this, in your kisses
And I will know,
When I am loving you

Fantasies capture reality
When I'm loving you
Every kiss, every touch
I'll replay for you
As it exist in my mind
When I'm making love to you

When looking for love

Have I left one stone unturned?
In search of a love my heart so yearns
Born alone, yet refuse to die
Without someone to lay by my side
Dear God I plead on hands and knees
Like the innocence of a newborn child
Reveal to me my heart's desire
A ray of light at the breaking dawn
Stretched across a misty lawn
The beauty of the sun as it sets
So is the love I long to posses
How long must I wait?
Questions foolishly asked, with no reply
As loneliness infects my smile
And the essence of life
develops a bitter taste
Am I doomed to forever waste?
Fall victim to the decomposition
of this tiresome chase
When looking for love where to begin?
Where to look? How long will it take?
Questions without answers
Love without a face

When the caged bird sings

When your eyes cry invisible tears
Rest assured that my heart hears
The sorrow no one else understands,
I feel
Even though we've
been separated for too many years
The song you sing still rings clear
If I could give you back
your flight I would
I just hope for now it's enough that
you're understood
What binds you may
or may not be for your own good
From your captivity take
what many never could
These bars that hold your physical
frame may restrain
But, only you can unlock
that which keeps you sane
The freedom you seek is yours to claim
Never ever let them see your fear
When your eyes cry invisible tears
Rest assured that my heart hears!
Sing caged bird, sing
Sing 'til your heart is content
Sing your frustrations

and all your regrets
Sing 'til there are no tears left
Sing until every encrypted note is told
Sing until your face, I behold

Wrong type of love

Some say it is wrong to love someone
that looks nothing like me
They taunt me with remarks
About how his ancestors
hung mine from trees
When I look in his eyes
that is not what I see
I am blind to the hatred
forged by years of bondage and
visions of southern cotton fields
Do I contemplate his use
of the word nigger?
Not when those of my race
use it to greet each other
Addressed to all sista's and brotha's
The love you label wrong
might just be the one you've given me
With distasteful, even profane nouns
you have labeled me your queen
Yet the authenticity of this throne
remains unseen, as if it's majestic

quality is make-believe
Cast your judgment wisely
or you too will be judged
The lynching you tell stories of
might just be a reflection of your hug
Consider the true meaning of,
the wrong type of love

YARDIE

"Rude bwoy, ya rememba, memba,
memba me lickle island Jamaica"
I'm a Jamaican living in America
Trying to dream that American dream
I gave up beef patties and coco bread
For apple pies and MTV
I used to listen to Bob Marley
And climb mango trees
Eating jerk fish and
hardo bread on the beach
Now I'm being tested in the streets
by Americans
that want to hear me speak
They say, you can't be Jamaican
you sound just like me
"Rude bwoy, ya rememba, memba,
memba me lickle island Jamaica"
And then I go back to Jamaica

only to face the same bullshit
Born, left when I was three
Now when I walk the streets
they call me Yankee
"Wa lon deh, nah badda disrespeck me
Caan you see sey, I and I a Yardie
Betta yet, a na un-nah same one a kill off
un-nah one anotha fi Tommy Hilifiger
an a run roun' a chat 'bout
that's my nigga!"
Is there something
missing in my swagger?
Or is it that you're jealous of me?
If I handed you my passport
To the land of "opportunity"
Will that appease?
Will you let me live?
Will you let me breath?
You call me Yankee
as if that's derogative
But, I can't tell by the way you live
the Kentucky Fried Chicken
you feed your kids
Honestly, it's easier
to get jerk chicken in New York
than it is in Kingston 3
"Rude bwoy, ya rememba, memba,
memba me lickle island Jamaica"

I'm tired of opening the newspaper
Reading about people selling weed
Deportees busting gunshots
And curfews locking down the streets
Listening to little kids
running around talking about
"A whey de bloodclot"
I miss the Jamaica I used to know
I miss those streets where I used to grow
the rhythm of reggae beats
that satisfy my soul
laying under the stars, on the beach,
as the breaking current wets my feet
You know, back when
I was known as a YARDIE

Yardie Enough

Will I ever be Jamaican enough
for those that judge my authenticity
by degrees of black, gold and green

Will I ever be real enough
to cook their ackee and saltfish
fry their dumplings in dozens
and pour their mint tea

Will they ever accept me for me
Navel string cut under coconut trees
Love me Yardie
Love me for me
Yankee accent and all
Cheeseburger eating me

Patois is not a fling
Not just a weekend thing
I try on when I walk down Eastern
Parkway
Flag swinging, jump and waving
Trying to get you to love me for me

I left when I was too young
to know what I was leaving

But the years have not caused this heart
from beating
With the rhythm of
that same lover's rock
That brought this soul into existence
But in your eyes
I will never be Yardie enough

I want to say thank you my friends and family for helping me walk through fire; words can't capture my gratitude for all that you have done and what you continue to do; I love you!

- *Aisha*

Family is everything…Al-Hamdulillah!

" *In life and love we meet triumphs and we meet defeats.
The words captured on these pages are reflections of
achievement, love, pain, sorrow and aspirations for a better
tomorrow.*" — *Aisha DaCosta* a.k.a **ADDicted**

"An important milestone in any poet's life is the first chapbook
they conjure into print. It announces and commemorates the
nights by the lamp reading and scribbling, and the sunrises of
inspiration that grew into a body of work. Congratulations to
Aisha on her arrival at this milestone." - Marc Smith, Author of
the "Complete Idiot's Guide to Slam Poetry"

www.ingramcontent.com/pod-product-compliance
Lightning Source LLC
Chambersburg PA
CBHW031328040426

42443CB00005B/257